The Pooh Party Book

Inspired by Winnie-The-Pooh and
The House at Pooh Corner by A. A. Milne

by Patsy Kumm
Illustrated by Ernest H. Shepard

With diagrams by Kenneth Ody

Methuen Children's Books · London

First published in Great Britain 1975
by Methuen Children's Books Ltd
11 New Fetter Lane, London EC4P 4EE

Individual copyright for text and illustrations:
Winnie-the-Pooh copyright 1926
The House at Pooh Corner copyright 1928
Text © 1975 by Patsy Kumm
Diagrams © 1975 by Methuen Children's Books Ltd.
All rights reserved
Printed in Great Britain by
Cox & Wyman Ltd, Fakenham, Norfolk

ISBN 0 416 78940 4

Contents

'Owl,' said Christopher Robin, *'I am going to give a party.'*
'You are, are you?' said Owl.
'And it's to be a special sort of party . . .'

Winnie-the-Pooh

Chapter One

Planning a Party

Giving a party can be a great deal of fun. It can be held to celebrate something special, or because it's a particular time of the year; or it can be a spur of the moment get-together with friends. But whatever the occasion you'll want it to go with a swing. And the nicest parties are usually those which have some careful planning behind them: ideas to get them going, and ideas for toning them down if they get too exuberant.

Ideally all the guests should go home feeling pleased with what they have contributed to the fun, and it is up to the hosts to give them a chance to show what they can do. But don't over-organize. If a game like Shipwrecks or Broadcasting (you'll find them in the Index at the end) is a great success, it can go on for longer than you expected, and then it is maddening to have to stop because Hide and Seek is next on the programme!

If you live in a flat or a semi-detached or terrace house, or if you intend to have your party in the garden, tell your neighbours in advance. Few people mind a noise provided they know it won't happen every day!

What kind of party? Indoors or out? For people of the same age, or the family kind for mixed ages? This last sort takes more organizing, because pencil and paper games that suit a seven-year-old are no good for a ten-year-old. On the other hand, even if you are ten or more you often enjoy playing games like Blind Man's Buff and pin the tail on Eeyore, if you know that later you can retreat upstairs to play records or organize a Quiz, while the younger ones paint happily downstairs.

If it's an indoor party, be quite certain how much of the house you can use, and mark clearly those rooms which are out of bounds. This prevents a raid on your mother's wardrobe when dressing up for Charades!

Even in summer you have to consider the weather and be prepared for a wet day (or a 'very Blusterous' one) that drives you indoors. This is when an attic, a play-room or even a large garage comes in useful. But if it is reasonably fine you can have an outdoor party even in winter, provided you warn your guests to come in their anoraks or macintoshes and Wellington boots. It's useful to have some old jerseys and jeans to lend to anyone who has come in their best clothes.

Some parties, of course, are arranged on the spur of the moment. You get up and see that it's a 'hummy sort of day outside and birds singing', and so you think it's just the day to go on a picnic. But this book is mostly about planned parties. Some ideas for these begin on page 13.

If there is a lot of preparation to be done – decorations to be made, for instance (see page 55) – you could have a pre-party get-together, asking your most nimble-fingered friends.

Getting Down To Details

How many friends to invite depends on space if it is an indoor party. If you are having a sit-down meal how many can you seat round your table or tables? Even if it is to be a sit-on-the-floor meal there is a limit to the number you can fit in.

When you have decided on the kind of party, check how many beakers, mugs, glasses, plates, knives, forks and spoons your home can provide, and where you can borrow more if need be. If you borrow, keep a list – it saves a lot of confusion after the party. Disposable plates etc. save washing up (and breakages) but cost money.

And that leads on to: how much can you afford to spend? You will have to buy food as well as extras like straws, balloons, prizes (these aren't essential but are much enjoyed), perhaps small gifts to take home, and possibly some equipment for games and for making things – pencils, adhesive etc. All this needs checking at least a week ahead, but once you have given one party you'll find you store away likely material ready for the next. Persuade your family to hoard!

It is handy to have a Dressing-up Box (better still, an old trunk – in the best story books of long ago there was always one in the attic) and a Bit Box. You can collect things over the months, ready for parties. Into the first you put any discarded clothes and material, preferably brightly coloured. Into the second go things that are often thrown away: paper bags, cardboard, scraps of material, Christmas cards, the carboard rolls from lavatory and kitchen paper, bits of string, cotton reels, milk bottle tops, yoghurt and margarine cartons and lids, wire clothes hangers and syrup tins. You can add pebbles, marbles, pine cones, tea-cards, feathers, a box of beads and another of buttons.

For paper and pencil games, hoard scrap paper too – anything that is blank on one side. It is surprising how much of this comes into every house and is often thrown straight into the waste-paper basket.

How Much Food

You will find out how to make a rough guess at what you will need on page 63, but it is hard to be exact, because on the one hand you may have a guest like Tigger, who only liked Extract of Malt; on the other, one like Pooh who was always ready for a little something.

Don't open your whole supply of things like crisps and pea-nuts at once. Keep some in reserve in case other food runs out. It is a help too to have some packets of sweet and savoury bis-cuits which could be taken back if you don't use them. Mark them clearly RESERVE SUPPLIES, NOT TO BE OPENED UNLESS NEEDED. This will keep at bay the enthusiastic helper who opens up every packet of crisps and biscuits in sight, so that your family is eating stale remains for weeks afterwards!

'There is an invitation for you.'
'What's that like?'
'An Invitation!'
'Yes, I heard you. Who dropped it?'
'This isn't anything to eat, it's
asking you to the party. Tomorrow.'
Winnie-the-Pooh

Invitations

You can use bought invitation cards, of course, but it is more fun to make your own, using a cardboard box or cereal packet cut up, or the plain backs of Christmas or birthday cards.

Suppose you decide on a Pooh Party. You can draw an outline of a honey pot or a picture of Pooh on a piece of card, then cut round the outline. Draw in the details and colour it. If there is room write your invitation on the picture, but if it is too small write on the back. The card must be small enough to fit into an envelope if it is to be posted, but if you are going to deliver it by hand you can make the invitation as large and unusual in shape as you like. Huge cards could be propped securely against friends' front doors, or tied to a branch of a tree where they are certain to be seen.

For a Nature Trail Party see the suggestion on page 16, and for an Ice-Cream Party see page 18. Invitations for a Cook-and-Eat Party could be shaped like a casserole or a frying-pan.

The invitation should read something like this:

Dear Sarah and Mike,
    We are having a Pooh Fancy Dress Party here
on January 6, from 2.30 to 5.30 p.m.
and hope you can both come.
    Jane and Jack

or

Dear Mary and Pete,
    Can you come to Brunch here
at 11 o'clock on Tuesday, August 12?
We hope to go for a long walk
afterwards. Please wear old clothes,
and Wellington boots if it is wet.
    Jill and David

Under the invitations put your address and R.S.V.P. which means *Répondez s'il vous plait* (French for 'Please reply').

Chapter Two

Some Party Themes

Christmas, birthdays, end of term, success in examinations, a welcome to new neighbours – there are endless reasons for giving a party. You could have a Space Age Party or a Circus Party – it's easy to see the possibilities in these. Here are a few more ideas that will suit all ages.

A Pooh Party

Each guest is given something to wear to indicate a Pooh character (see pages 49-51 for costume ideas). To decorate the room make a tree (using a large branch from the garden or cardboard etc.) over the doorway, and this can be Pooh's house. If you have a hatch into the kitchen, make this the entrance to Pooh's house instead, and serve ice-cream or even a meal through it. Decorate the rest of the room with greenery to look like the forest.

You will want to play more than Pooh games, but 'Pinning the Tail on Eeyore' (see page 27) is a must, and if you have a Quiz some of the questions could have a Pooh slant, like 'What was the name of Kanga's baby?' and 'Whose house was at Pooh Corner?' (and just in case you don't know, the answers are Roo and Eeyore!)

'Friends,' he said, 'including
oddments, it is a great pleasure,
or perhaps I had better say
it has been a pleasure so far, to
see you at my party. . . .'
Winnie-the-Pooh

An Easter Party

Primroses and other spring flowers, and fluffy chicks are all you need for table decorations, with perhaps Easter bunnies for place-markers, unless you are going to paint or decorate Easter eggs beforehand. Most guests like the fun of painting eggs to take home, and some ideas for this are on page 92.

If you are going to have an Easter egg hunt, you can either hide a lot of little chocolate eggs and let the guests keep all they find (making sure that the smallest children get their share by perhaps giving them a special place to look), or put a name on each, rather bigger, egg, and let each guest find the right one, keeping very quiet about it and leaving it undisturbed, if the wrong one is discovered. If the weather is fine and dry, eggs can be hidden in the garden, within reach of paths.

A Nursery Rhyme Party

Fancy dress should be optional, but young children of four or so love to come as Little Miss Muffet or Little Boy Blue.

If there's an artist in the family decorate the room with scenes from nursery rhymes: Little Bo-Peep and her sheep etc.

An alternative would be a series of mobiles (see page 94) made from wire clothes hangers, from each of which dangled on fine wire or heavy thread the characters in a nursery rhyme. 'The

House that Jack Built', 'The Old Woman Who Lived in a Shoe', 'Pussy Cat, Pussy Cat, Where Have You Been?' 'Mary, Mary, Quite Contrary', 'Hey Diddle Diddle' – all these would make excellent mobiles or pictures, and singing or saying the songs or verses would make a good start to the party. So would the singing game 'Here We Go Round the Mulberry Bush'.

A Puppet Show

If some of your friends have puppets they would probably like a chance to give a show. Prepare a suitable table, and set the ball rolling with a show of your own puppets.

A Brunch Party

This is a breakfast-and-lunch party, and the best time to start it is at about eleven o'clock. It's a particularly good idea if you are going on a long walk afterwards and don't want to carry a picnic with you. It suits those who have slept late and haven't had time for breakfast, and those who got up early and are more than ready for elevenses.

Put a selection of cereals, a jug of milk and a bowl of sugar on the table, with a dish of stewed apple or other fruit you have cooked the day before. Buy a French or a long white loaf and at the last moment cut it into pieces (it goes stale quickly). Provide rolls or white and brown bread, butter, marmalade, jam and honey. Check to see if you may cook something, and then prepare a big dish of bacon, sausages and tomatoes baked in the oven. You might also have some baked beans heated in a saucepan. Packets of potato crisps are a useful stand-by. Serve the hot food straight on to the plates in the kitchen to ensure fair shares!

If it's a hot day serve fruit drinks (see Chapter Five). If it's cold offer a choice of tea or hot chocolate.

Provided the sun is shining this is the kind of meal that can be eaten in the garden in winter or summer.

A Nature Trail Party

As an invitation, send each guest a small notebook (made by yourself) with the Nature Trail invitation written on the cover. Tell your friends to bring the notebooks with them (but have one or two spare ones in case they forget.)

Pack a picnic bag or box for each guest with perhaps sandwiches, hard-boiled eggs, pickles and crisps or the Picnic Tubs (see Chapter Five).

Set off to a destination chosen beforehand which offers a lot in the way of nature interest. The place can be somewhere no great distance from home; the local park or recreation ground, a piece of waste land – or even the churchyard if you have permission. It's surprising how much wild life you can find in the middle of a town, if it is not possible to take a country walk. Or take a bus and *then* a walk.

When you arrive, give each guest a pencil to go with the notebook, and a list of things to find and do, like:
List all the flowers you can find, and draw one or two of them.
What sort of tree have you seen most often today? Draw a leaf.
Pick four different grasses and draw them.
Name three birds you have seen here.

Make a list of any sounds you have heard on the Nature Trail –
including such things as aeroplanes, a motor-mower, the fall of
a leaf, a dog barking, the song of a robin etc.

You could make it a competition and give a prize to the one
who produces the best notebook at the end of the expedition.

An Ice-cream Party

Invitation cards could be in the shape of an ice-cream cornet. Colour them in pale ice-cream shades, and write your invitations on them.

Even at an Ice-Cream Party though, you need a foundation of something more solid. (Chapter Five has some suggestions.)

When your guests have eaten their first course, take the ice-cream from the freezer and tip it into bowls at the last minute. Hand each guest a small bowl, and let them all create their own individual mixtures by helping themselves to ice-cream and to a row of dishes of assorted nuts, chopped up fruit (such as tinned apricots and peaches) or fresh fruit in season, like strawberries and raspberries, syrups (made from sweetened fruit juice), whipped cream, jam and chocolate chips.

This is quite an expensive party, and it could perhaps be combined with some festive occasion like a birthday.

A Barbecue Party

An outdoor barbecue is possible even without expensive equipment, but you need some grown-up help. You will want a cooker grill to cook the food on (an old one, *not* the one from the family cooker!), charcoal and something to burn this in. If someone will lend you an old metal wheelbarrow (say what you need it for) half-fill it with pebbles or stones before adding the charcoal and putting the grill on top. Or you can punch holes in the sides of a big biscuit tin (for ventilation), put a layer of charcoal in the bottom, and again use a cooker grill as grid on which to put the sausages, chicken pieces, hamburgers or whatever is to be cooked.

Remember that the tin will get very hot – don't stand it on a wooden trestle table, for example.

Remember, too, that the charcoal can be difficult to get going – it needs gentle fanning. Bellows are ideal, but you can fan with a folded newspaper. It's no good trying to cook food over the charcoal until it has all become glowing and red hot.

Keep small children from coming too near, and when the food is cooked don't let them help themselves from the barbecue.

You could put out a selection of relishes such as chopped onion, tomato sauce, or chutney and guests can add what they like to their own food.

A Soup-and-Snow Winter Woozle Party

This would have to be a spur-of-the-moment party after a heavy fall of snow. Prepare a quick and easy meal which can be reheated, such as savoury sausages or scrambled eggs. Have your friends gather at your house at, say, eleven in the morning before going somewhere where the snow is still untrodden – in your own garden if it is big enough, or in a near-by park.

It's fun to make Woozle tracks like Pooh and Piglet, either following one another round and round a tree, or perhaps dividing up, each going to a corner of the untrodden snow (keeping to the edge so that you don't spoil it with footprints until you are ready) and then racing one another diagonally across it. Build a snowman, play at snowballs. Then head for home and some piping hot soup.

An After-the-Show Party

This is really just a meal and a chance to talk about what you have seen – whether it's pantomime, a play or a visit to the cinema. No special decorations are needed, but plenty to eat – and especially savoury things like Little Meat Balls on page 65 if you have eaten sweets in the intervals.

A Cook-and Eat Party

This can only be a small party, unless you have an enormous farmhouse kitchen. Keep the food simple. Get all the ingredients and equipment ready beforehand.

When your guests arrive plan with them what job each will do. Say it's to be hot dogs. One cooks the sausages, another chops onions, another fries them. One person slits and butters rolls – and so on. And if one friend is hopeless at cooking, that one can take the ice-cream from the freezer and divide it up.

A Bring-a-Friend Party

This speaks for itself but is a good idea, for instance, on a new housing estate.

For very small children the 'friend' could be a Teddy or doll, with a warm welcome for each.

A Pirate Party

Tell your friends to come dressed as pirates. This needs nothing elaborate: a black patch fixed over one eye with elastic or sticking plaster, a coloured scarf tied rakishly on the head, huge rings dangling from ears, T-shirt and jeans, with another scarf round the waist – and cardboard or wooden swords and cutlasses painted silver, or covered in silver paper.

Divide guests into two teams, each with a different-coloured skull and crossbones flag. Give each team the name of a ship and let them compete against each other in games.

This party can include Shipwrecks (see page 38), and is fun indoors or out.

A Hallowe'en Party

This should be on October 31. In the old Celtic calendar it was the last day of the year, when witches and warlocks held their revels. Your invitations could show a witch on a broomstick, and decorations should be as spooky as possible: dangling spiders, black cats, a skeleton or two, an evil eye perhaps. A log fire is ideal, with the room lit only by night-lights firmly fixed in large, hollowed-out swedes or turnips, on which grotesque faces are painted (your family will have to eat a lot of mashed swede to use up what you cut out!) Apple Bobbing (see page 33) is a traditional game, followed by roasting chestnuts in the fire, and baked potatoes should form part of the meal.

Best of all, as you sit round the fire, someone should tell or read a really creepy ghost story. Perhaps you could contrive a few 'noises off' at the end of this: some eerie howls, clanking of chains, a baying dog. And you can buy some very realistic snakes to produce at the right moment!

If you and your friends want to dress up, old white sheets or dust-sheets make good ghost costumes, and anything black or

dark makes cloaks for witches and warlocks. Tall hats for both are easy to make with cardboard, gum and black paint or paper. Those for witches have brims, those for warlocks should be dotted with cut-out stars, moons and other shapes (see page 33).

Chapter Three

Games

In each section – *Indoor Games* and *Outdoor Games* – those suggested for younger children come first though many are enjoyed by all ages. Of course many indoor games can be played outdoors, and *vice versa*; but a strenuous tug-of-war, for instance, can be a disaster in a small room, while games with pencil and paper are awkward played in the garden on a windy day.

Here is one game to break the ice, indoors or out, if some of your guests don't know one another.

The Other Half

Collect or draw pictures of animals or things (a horse, a table, an elephant, a snake – or, if it is a Pooh Party, any of the characters in the Pooh Books). Stick or draw the pictures on stiff paper or card and cut in half. Mix up the halves and hand one to each guest on arrival. In finding their 'other half' the ice is broken.

For older children you could divide proverbs like 'A rolling stone / gathers no moss', or the names of familiar television comedians who work in pairs.

*'Tigger, Tigger, we're going
to jump! Look at me jumping,
Tigger! Like flying, my jumping
will be. Can Tiggers do it?'*
The House at Pooh Corner

Indoor Games

Pinning the Tail on Eeyore

Draw a large picture of Eeyore on a piece of stiff card or plywood. Colour him grey. Draw his tail separately on paper, or make it of string or wool or plaited raffia, with a tassel at the end.

Hang the picture on the wall and mark on it where the tail should go. Blindfold the players in turn, and give them the tail plus a drawing pin. As each pins the tail on Eeyore, mark round the pinpoint with a ring and put the player's initials. The winner is the one who places the tail most accurately.

Musical Bumps with Cushions

Put cushions on the floor – one less than the number of players. Everyone walks briskly round the cushions to the music of piano, radio or record player – or even to the sound of someone energetic saying 'pom-diddy-pom-pom' over and over again. When the sound stops, everyone tries to sit on a cushion. The one who doesn't is out of the game. One cushion is removed, the sound starts again. . . . and so on until one cushion is left with two people competing for it.

The Search for Small

Small was a very tiny insect who was lost but found by Winnie-the-Pooh, after everyone had searched and searched. In this game any small object can be Small. All but one player sit in a circle. One player stands in the middle with eyes closed, and counts up to twenty while the others are passing Small from hand to hand around the circle. On 'twenty' the centre player can look and try to guess where Small is hiding. If the guess is correct the centre player changes places with the one hiding Small, or the game continues until he is found.

Pass the Parcel

Before the party wrap up a present – perhaps, as at the party Christopher Robin gave for Pooh, a Special Pencil Case. Then wrap the parcel in another layer of paper (it can be newspaper) with another small present – an uninflated balloon, a marble, a tiny bag of sweets. After each item wrap the parcel again, with plenty of paper, securely tied or taped, until you have a big parcel.

All guests sit in a circle. Music is played and the parcel passed from hand to hand. When the music stops in mid-tune, whoever is holding the parcel undoes as much as possible but must pass it on at once when the music starts again. Whoever unwraps a present keeps it, until finally the last present is unwrapped. A fairly brisk tune adds to the fun!

This can also be played with only *one* present – right in the middle of layers of wrapping, each layer firmly tied or stuck.

Beat the Pan

This is a good game for the end of a party because everyone wins something. It can be a way to give each guest a going home gift as well. A sturdy kitchen pan is placed upside-down in the centre of the room and under it is placed a small prize. In turn, each player is blindfolded and given a wooden spoon, then turned round and round. Either crouching or on all fours, the player tries to first find and then to beat the pan, with everyone encouraging and directing from the sidelines. When a player beats the pan the blindfold is removed and the prize won. Another prize is then placed under the pan until everyone has had a turn.

Dress the Doll

You need one doll for each two guests. Each doll should have the same number of items of clothing.

Players form pairs, each with a doll and its clothing. On the word 'Go' each pair has to dress the doll but using one hand only – the other hand must be kept behind the back. The winners are the pair who dress the doll first.

Spider Web

Tie long pieces of string to small presents and hide them. Wind the strings about the room, overlapping them. Then with a clothes peg, clip the end of each string, with the name of a child, to a curtain, cushion, armchair – anywhere easily visible. Guests find their names and follow the string back to the presents, winding it on the clothes peg – getting very tangled up with the web and each other as they do so!

Trundle the Trencher

Sit in a ring on the floor with one in the middle who spins a tin plate, a round biscuit-tin lid or, best of all, a round wooden breadboard. As he spins he calls out a name, and that person must leap up and catch the 'trencher' before it stops spinning. If he fails he must pay a forfeit, named by the spinner: a choice perhaps of singing the verse of a song, saying the alphabet backwards, or not smiling for a minute. If the player manages this, he then spins the trencher. If he fails, he goes back to the ring.

The circle should be a really large one to make the game exciting. If it's on the small side, make a rule that the person whose name is called has to run behind the one next to him on his way to catch the 'trencher'.

Matchbox Derby

For this you need six empty matchboxes and six of those whistle-blowers that shoot out when you blow and make a high-pitched noise.

Put the six matchboxes along the edge of a table, give six guests a blower each, and let the opposite edge of the table be the finish. The first to push the matchbox to the finish with the blower is the winner.

You could have only three matchboxes and blowers, and have heats of three people at a time, with a final champions' race for the winners of each of the heats.

Balloon Race

Put a pile of uninflated balloons at one end of the room, with lengths of string or thread to tie them when blown up. At a given signal the guests rush to the balloons, blow them up fully,

tie them, then 'head' them from a starting line to the finishing line. Fallen balloons may be placed on the head by hand, but hands must not be used to propel them!

Sometimes balloons are hard to blow up. It's a good idea to blow them up beforehand (a special balloon pump makes it easier) and then deflate them. Once they have been blown up, it won't be so difficult a second time round.

Thistle

Provide every player with a raw potato, a saucer of pins and a pair of gloves. Wearing the gloves, players must pick up the pins one at a time and stick them into the potato. The winner is the one who, at the end of three minutes, has the greatest number of pins in his potato, thereby making the best prickly 'thistle'.

Fish Race

Cut out fish shapes from thin paper – all the same length (not less than 6 inches). Draw in their eyes etc. and paint them different colours.

Guests must fan them from starting to finishing post, using a folded newspaper.

Funny Hats

Prepare for each guest a package of coloured paper, pins or sticky tape, and trimmings: feathers, scraps of material etc. In a given time each guest makes a hat, and wears it in a parade when everyone can choose the winner.

Apple Bobbing

This is a game for Hallowe'en. It is most fun if several players take part at once, but this can mean a good deal of spilt water, so it's best played in the kitchen. You need a bath or large bowl of water. Float your apples and let three people at a time kneel down and try to pick an apple out with their teeth. The first to do so is the winner and goes on to the next round, or the winner can be the one who picks most apples out in a given time.

A variation of this is Bobbing for Fortunes. Prepare 'fortunes' on slips of paper and wrap each in plastic, sealed with sticky tape. Cut slits in enough apples for all the guests and stick the fortunes in them. Float the apples in water. The players have to pick out their fortunes with their teeth, and when they have done so they read them aloud, so the funnier you make the fortunes the better the entertainment.

Bun Bobbing

Stretch a cord between two chairs. From it hang small buns on strings with a really big knot at the bottom. Players must eat the whole bun. If any of it (except crumbs) falls to the ground, they are disqualified. A dust sheet is advisable for this game!

Calling the Tune

One person, using the fingertips of one or both hands, 'plays' the tune of a song on any hard surface – table, tray, biscuit-tin or drum. Start with something simple like 'Baa-baa, black sheep' or a hymn like 'Onward, Christian soldiers'. It is surprising how quickly you become skilful enough to play (and to recognize) your favourite classical, jazz or pop music. The first to guess the tune plays the next one.

Twenty Objects

Bring in, covered, a tray of different small objects: an egg-cup, pencil, spoon, tin of shoe polish, ash-tray, lipstick, marble – familiar things like that. Let everyone look for a moment or two, then cover again. For small children ten objects are enough, and if they can't write they can draw their answers. For older people, have twenty objects. The winner is the one who writes down the names of all the items.

Back and Front

Two equal teams face each other. At one end of the line are two bowls with six small objects in each: marble, matchbox, button, penny, pea, bean, for instance. At a signal the player next the bowl picks up each object in turn and passes it down the line. The last player returns the object, but this time it goes *behind* the line. This may mean that players are passing objects in front of them and behind them at the same time! The winning team is the one getting all six items back in the bowl first.

Charades

These can be either mimed or spoken. Best of all, you can dress up for them – but for this you must allow a good deal of time. For the simplest miming, two of you choose a word – e.g. *hamster* – and mime cutting ham to make sandwiches, followed by stirring a cake. Then, on all fours, the two do their best to run about like hamsters!

The spoken kind of charade needs more planning. Any number of people can act out the syllables, but you must decide beforehand who is actually going to say each syllable, bringing it into a conversation. Finally you bring in the whole word, e.g. *porc-u-pine*, which would therefore need four different 'scenes'.

Whichever kind of charade you choose, someone must announce, before you begin, how many syllables are in the word.

And Then . . .

'Peter and Jane were sitting on one of the seats in the shopping centre waiting for their mother when suddenly. . . .' Someone starts a story, the next person continues it until everyone has had a turn. The last must give the story an ending – and very sudden that ending frequently is, if the last person is left with a very complicated situation, and so finishes up with something like 'Then they all got on a train and went to Scotland.' You can vary this game by giving everyone a second turn, or make it more exciting by letting one person call out the name of the one who is to continue.

Which Baby Were You?

Ask your guests to bring photographs of themselves when they were babies. Pin these up, each clearly numbered (you can sticky-tape numbers to them without damaging the photographs). Hand each guest a sheet of paper with the numbers listed, and a pencil, and tell them to put the right name against each number. Then read out the correct list.

Shadowgraph

Stretch a white sheet across the room with a bright light a yard or so behind it. Performers go in turn behind the sheet, so that the light throws their shadow on it, and whoever in the audience guesses what they are miming has the next turn. Two people can mime together if they prefer this.

Suggestions for subjects to mime: boxing, playing football, asking for forgiveness (kneel sideways to the screen, and bow with outstretched hands to the floor), flying a kite, eating.

It isn't easy to remember that what you are aiming at is a clear silhouette, but a little practice soon makes perfect.

Telegrams

Someone reads out a number of letters, e.g. MLIBSHDGCP, from which everyone composes a telegram using each letter to begin a word, such as 'Mary Lost In Balloon Send Helicopter Dinner Getting Cold Philip'. The more absurd the telegram the better. When all have written one, the telegrams are read out.

Whispers

Sit in a ring. One person whispers to the next a sentence like 'Did you know that a man from the moon landed on our lawn last night?' The next person whispers it quickly to the next, and so on round the circle. No one, of course, must ask for the sentence to be repeated. The last person says what he *thinks* he has heard, and compares this with what the actual sentence was. As with all games of this kind, it needs to be played quickly.

Broadcasting

Let someone pretend to be an announcer either on radio or television. If the latter, devise an oblong 'screen' through which to speak and be seen, using a clothes-horse, an old picture frame or a small table plus dust-sheets or rugs – anything that blocks out the speaker except for head and shoulders. Start off with the weather and some local made-up news, perhaps, followed by an interview with a second person on something topical. Guests may be a bit nervous at first, but it is surprising how much talent can be revealed when they 'have a go' – and then the problem often is how to stop them! Hosts should think up a few subjects beforehand, and perhaps speak first before they are elbowed away from the 'box'!

Shipwrecks

This needs space and solid, not-too-precious furniture! It can also be played outdoors, or best of all in a barn.

Players must get from ship to shore without falling in the water – that is, they must get from base to home without touching the ground: over furniture (socks or bare feet here), jumping from rug to rug, climbing on biscuit-tins etc. Anyone who touches the ground is out, but if it is a mixed-ages party, the little ones can be helped. Ideally, a picnic meal is eaten at the end.

The game could be played as Pooh's Expotition to the North Pole, with a suitable flag awaiting the explorers at the end of it.

Picture-making (Collage)

Provide lots of oddments – scraps of material, cotton wool, toothpicks, macaroni, lentils, buttons, chips of cork, string, dried everlasting flowers, silver and gold foil, small pine cones, Christmas cards, ribbon and anything else you can find in your store of such things. You will also need some large, stiff sheets of paper, good strong gum or glue, some needles and thread, and at least one pair of scissors.

Spread out your materials, and let guests help themselves, perhaps limiting them at first to three items. With these they begin a picture, sticking objects on to the paper, and sewing fabrics together if they need to do this to create special effects. They help themselves to more materials as their pictures take shape.

After a time limit – say half an hour – you can have a picture show and decide whose picture is best.

Quiz

This needs preparation beforehand. The kind of quiz depends on your friends. If, like Owl, they are no good at spelling (he, you may remember, could 'spell his own name WOL, yet somehow went all to pieces over delicate words like MEASLES and BUTTERED-TOAST') then you won't ask them to spell 'harass' and 'embarrass'. Make up a wide variety of questions so that those who prefer reading to watching television can answer 'Who wrote *Vanity Fair*?' even if they don't know the names of current television

characters. Think up questions about winners in sport, and general information ('What happened in London in 1666?').

Give each guest paper and pencil. Read out the questions slowly, then read out the correct answers and find out who has got most right.

You may prefer to have two teams, with someone not in either team who gives the questions and keeps the score.

What Nonsense!

Prepare beforehand a tale (or use one you already know like 'The Babes in the Wood') and put some nonsense sentences into it like 'It was a fine summer's day and after their picnic the children played snowballs'. Or, 'As we walked to the cottage at the bottom of the hill, we puffed and panted because the climb was so steep.' At each 'nonsense' players have to shout 'No'. It is more exciting if you divide people into two teams, and keep count of which team shouts first.

WOL

Pretend You're a Poet

Four words are called out – say, *last*, *tree*, *flower* and *bird*. Everyone has to make up an eight-line poem in which four lines end with these words, and each of the other four must rhyme, i.e. they could end, for instance, with *fast*, *bee*, *shower* and *heard*. After perhaps ten minutes, the folded poems are put in a bowl, and each person picks out one to read aloud. You can vote which is the winner, or just enjoy the fun of hearing what others have made up.

*'I've got an idea,' said Rabbit, 'and here it is. We take Tigger for
a long explore somewhere where he's never been,
and we lose him there, and next morning we find him again.'*
The House at Pooh Corner

Outdoor Games

Tail Tag

You need a length of rope long enough for all players to hold it
with about two feet between them. The leader has to try to catch
the one at the tail end of the rope. When this happens, the leader
becomes the tail, the second person becomes the leader and so on,
until the last one is leader.

It's a lot of fun, because of course, the tail has to try (without
letting go of the rope) *not* to be caught.

Washing Day

Tie two lengths of cord to trees or chairs to make two washing
lines at the right height for your guests. Under each put a basket
of 'washing' – say two dusters, two pairs of socks, six handker-
chiefs: the same in each container. Put a bowl of pegs under each
clothes line.

Divide your guests into two equal teams, and keep them all
behind a starting line. At a signal the first from each team runs
forward and pins the clothes on the line, then runs back; the next
in each team runs to the line and unpins the clothes, putting them
back into the basket. This continues at speed until all have had a
turn. The winning team is the one which finishes first.

You must explain before you begin that each sock and handkerchief must be pegged separately, a pair of socks counting as two items, not one.

Ankle Race

All players bend over and grasp their ankles with their hands. In this position they waddle – and waddle's the only word for it! – as fast as they can to the finishing line.

Statues

One player stands with his back to the others and some distance away from them. The rest move towards him slowly, and every time he turns round they freeze into statue positions: arms outstretched, one leg bent and so on. Anyone who wobbles is out! When the player turns his back the rest move forward again, until finally someone touches him. The last minutes of this game can be very exciting.

Howl, Dog, Howl

This is a noisy game, only to be played if you get on very well with the people who live near you!

Everyone stands in a circle, takes as deep a breath as possible, and then howls – *Wow, wow, wow, wow* – for as long as possible *without taking another breath*. The last one to keep howling wins.

Matchbox Collection

Hand everyone an empty matchbox. Give a time limit of perhaps ten minutes to collect and put in it as many different things as possible: tiny stone, flower petal, feather, seed, blade of grass etc. There mustn't be more than one of anything. The tinier the items the more can be squeezed in – and the winner is the one with the most.

Bucket Ball

Give two people six balls each – rubber or tennis balls, with a cross in colour to distinguish one set of six from the other. Put a bucket between them, and see who can bounce all six balls into the bucket first. The winner then takes on another player.

Eeyore's House

This needs a good deal of garden material like tree prunings, bamboos or bean poles, and other material like bracken or reeds gathered on country walks. You can either make one Eeyore house, or have a competition and make two, which is not only more exciting but leaves you with two houses to play in.

It is a good idea to do some preparation before your party –

'We will build an Eeyore House
with sticks at Pooh Corner for Eeyore.'
The House at Pooh Corner

apart from collecting the material. Drive six bamboo or bean poles into the ground, crossing at the top, to form the framework of each house. Divide all other material, including some lengths of string, into two heaps. At a signal both teams start, tying sticks horizontally to the framework, and interweaving twigs and bracken etc. till the house is complete and all material used up.

Potato Race

Choose six equal-sized potatoes. Six players, with the potatoes held in spoons, race from starting to finishing line, where they transfer their potatoes to spoons held by their opposite numbers (without touching the potatoes with their hands) who then race back to the starting point.

Wheelbarrow Race

This can only be played on grass! One player is the wheelbarrow, walking on the hands, while legs are held by the other player.

Mini-stilt Race

For this you need to save up empty tin cans beforehand. Syrup tins with lids are excellent if you can get enough of them, and they have no jagged edges. Punch a hole in each side of the can, near the top. Take 48 inch lengths of thick string and make a knot at one end. Thread the other end through a hole in the can, and make another knot, a big one, so that string cannot be pulled out of the can. Do the same with the hole on the other side of the can. You could paint each pair of cans a different colour.

For the race, each player stands on a pair of cans, holding the two strings tightly so that the can is lifted with each step taken. At a signal the players move from the starting line towards the finishing line. Anyone who falls off and puts a foot to the ground must go back to the start. Practice is advisable, but once you get the knack of it you soon progress from walking to running.

Jumping Race
Ankles are tied loosely with a scarf. At a signal players jump from
starting to finishing line.

Another jumping race, with no tying needed, for those with
too much energy: players jump up and down and up and down,
and see who can keep it up longest.

'I'm Pooh,' said Pooh.
'I'm Tigger,' said Tigger.
The House at Pooh Corner

Chapter Four

Party Wear and Decorations
Pooh Costumes

Fancy dress is fun, and although not every family has time or
talent to make costumes which will be worn once only, some
Pooh characters can be very simply made. Christopher Robin, for

example, needs little more than shorts, a shirt and sandals, plus a
soft hat. Or when guests arrive you could give them all ears and
a tail to show which of the Pooh book characters they are.

Ears are surprisingly easy to make (see page 78). Take an oblong piece of thin card, an inch or so longer than the ear you are making. Fold it in half lengthwise, and shape the ear – long and narrow for Rabbit, short and round for Pooh etc. Fold as shown in the diagram on page 79, and staple or stitch to a band of stiff material or card, and fasten as indicated. Paint the ears the appropriate colour, or glue soft material over them. Eeyore's ears must be floppy, so should be made entirely of material to the same pattern as Rabbit's.

Rabbit's tail could be made of cotton wool glued to a round of material to which a safety pin has already been attached with sticky tape. The tail is then pinned in place.

For Eeyore's tail, stuff part of the leg of a pair of old tights with cut-up old stockings, dip in coffee or a dye or poster paint, dry and add a tassel. Tigger would have a similar tail, but without a

tassel, dyed yellow (onion skins are useful for making the dye) and striped with dark poster paint.

If you want more 'dressing' up for a Pooh Party, most households could supply a striped T-shirt for Piglet, and perhaps a yellow jersey for Pooh – padded with cushions at front and back, these held in place with wide tape or material over each shoulder, safety-pinned to make them removable if Pooh gets too hot!

Kanga could wear a large rounded apron (see page 80) made of an old white sheet, with a pocket to fit the lower half. If you happened to have a toy kangaroo to put into the pocket, it would make it even clearer who she is!

For an owl costume you make a mask out of a paper bag. The kind with a gusset is best (see page 81). Try it on over your head to find out where to cut holes for eyes, nose and mouth. Then take it off and draw Owl's face. You could also make a wide circular collar of brown paper, (see page 81) and draw feathers on it with a felt pen, or make separate paper feathers and stick them on. If you are feeling ambitious you could make it full-length.

Party Hats

Margarine containers, round or oblong, make very jaunty hats (see page 82). Make two holes on either side and thread elastic through, knotted at each end. The elastic should fit comfortably under the chin. If the containers are plain, decorate them by drawing patterns with a felt-tipped pen, or sticking on coloured motifs. Write each guest's name on a hat. The containers could be covered with silver foil, with a gold star in front. They could have a tassel on top, or hanging down one side. This is made by fringing and rolling a strip of crepe paper and tying it with coloured cord.

Paper hats (see page 83) are easy to make, and a party table looks gay if there is one by each guest's plate. Cut strips of paper (crepe is stronger than plain) 7 or 8 inches deep and long enough to go round your head, with an overlap for gumming to form a circle. Before you gum, cut along the upper edge into points to look like a crown, or fringe the edge and turn it down. These are basic designs, but there is endless scope for variety. You could stick coloured gummed shapes round the hat. It should fit fairly loosely on the head – this allows for someone else's head being a bit larger than your own!

For a Hallowe'en Party you need witches' and warlocks' hats (see page 86). Try them first in newspaper. In fact, painted newspaper – two sheets gummed together to give strength – makes excellent hats. For each hat you need a quarter of a circle of paper. Cut a 15 inch square of paper. Take a piece of string 15 inches long, pin or hold it at one corner of the paper and swing the other end of the string in an arc, marking the curve with a pencil. Cut out and make a cone, joining the straight edges together with tape. Try it on your head. If it fits too loosely you can overlap the edges or cut a piece off. And if it is too small, which is unlikely, you try again with a 16 inch square!

For the brim you need a large circle. If you haven't got a suitable tray or waste-paper basket about 15 inches in diameter to use as pattern, use a dustbin lid and cut away about 2 inches all round the resulting circle of paper. Using a pudding basin for guide, cut a 5 inch hole in the centre, and snip inwards all round this hole. Turn up these snipped portions. You'll have to experiment to get the snips the right length, but they should not be less than 1 inch – preferably more. The brim of the hat should be about 3 inches wide, and the snipped portions are gummed into the inside of the cone.

Paint the hats black, or gum black paper over them, and decorate with signs suggesting witchcraft: new moons, stars, black cats and so on.

Warlocks wear hats without brims. Brims are for witches!

'. . . You know what I told you yesterday about making faces. If you go on making faces like Piglet's, you will grow up to look *like Piglet – and* then *think how sorry you will be.'*
Winnie-the-Pooh.

Masks

Domino masks (see page 87) are simplest of all to make and can be worn at all kinds of parties, such as Pirate and Hallowee'n. They often help to make a shy guest feel at home, because of course they are a kind of disguise. They can be made of thin card, painted and decorated, of stiff paper, of felt – anything firm enough to keep its shape. Make a hole at each end and fasten round the head with elastic or with tape or string tied at the back. Black dominoes look sinister. Those covered in gold or silver foil or decorated with tinsel and 'glitter' are very glamorous.

Bigger masks to cover the whole face can be made of paper bags, of stout paper, thin card or even of large picnic plates (see page 87). Cut holes for eyes, nose and mouth, and add decorations to suit the character you have in mind. For Rabbit, for instance, you could glue on pipe cleaners for whiskers; for a villainous pirate you could paint or stick on bristling eyebrows and moustache. Paper-bag masks cover the whole head and so need no fixing, but others have a hole at each side so that elastic or tape can be threaded through, to hold them in place. A lot of ingenuity can go into making masks. Do not use plastic bags, however.

'Yes, I just said to myself coming along:
'I wonder if Christopher Robin has such a thing
as a balloon about him?" I just said it to myself,
thinking of balloons, and wondering.'
Winnie-the-Pooh

Party Decorations

For an indoor party it's a good thing to think of balloons – they
always look festive. So do the traditional decorations for a
Christmas party of paper chains, holly and ivy, tinsel and glitter,
stars, shining balls and bells. But you will want other ideas for
parties with a particular theme.

Friezes

Fold long strips of paper concertina-wise (see page 88). On the
top section draw a character (a Pooh character for a Pooh Party,
a lamb, a rabbit, a witch, or a pirate, for other kinds of parties).
Make sure that at least some part of what you draw touches the
paper at each side. Carefully cut round the picture – but *not*
round that part of the outline which actually touches the two
edges of the paper. Then, when you spread the frieze out, you'll
have a whole row of characters linked together.

If you use coloured paper and an easily recognised shape –
like a cat (black paper would be good here), a witch, or Pooh
himself – the frieze could just be a silhouette. But in most cases

you would need to fill in the details and colour each character. It doesn't take long with a felt pen.

Small friezes could be pinned round cakes or lampshades, or used to decorate the tablecloth; larger ones could be hung round the mantelpiece or from strings as one hangs Christmas cards.

If you don't cut away the bottom of the paper but leave a flat base, you can fasten your friezes in circles so that they stand up and you could use tape to secure them to the table.

Place-markers

There's something really partyish about looking for your name at the place where you are going to sit, and place-markers can carry out the party theme (see page 90).

Cut pieces of thin cardboard measuring about 2 by 5 inches. Fold in half, with fold at top. Draw and colour an appropriate picture on the front, and write the guest's name inside, or you could use scissors to cut the place-marker into a special shape. For a Pirate Party you could have a skull and crossbones!

The Festive Table

A plain tablecloth can look partified with very little effort. Cut long strips of coloured crepe paper and pin them, either flat or twisted spirally, diagonally across the table. You could pin more strips in the opposite direction, making diamond-shaped spaces on which to stand the food. Bright colours are best for winter parties, pale ones for, say, an Easter Party when spring flowers are on the table.

Small children love to take home a posy of flowers, and if you have a garden, and if it is the right season you could put one by each place. They can be very small posies, with stems wrapped in wet cotton wool or paper, covered in foil so that the flowers don't wilt.

At a Christmas or Birthday Party the iced cake is usually the centrepiece of the table, but for other parties you will need more ideas (see page 91). Depending on the size and shape of the table, your base could be an old tray, a piece of wood or stout card, or a big dinner plate. A handbag mirror makes a good lake, and greenery for trees can be stuck in plasticine. You could make a road scene, using tiny model cars and a miniature garage, or a farmyard, or a snow scene, with igloos perhaps. These are easily made by drying (in the airing cupboard, or in the oven when it is cooling after cooking) the two halves of an orange from which you have scooped out the contents. Then cover them with adhesive and cotton wool, and put them near your lake in a snow scene made of white detergent powder mixed with water. Try a tablespoonful of detergent first, and see how far it goes, spreading it over stones or round bits of rock to give a hilly effect or for making an igloo in a winter scene. A cake-decoration sledge and polar bear would look attractive, and you could arrange ivy or other greenery round the edge of the plate or tray to make a decorative finish.

Easter Eggs

Eggs should be simmered slowly for half an hour, then put in cold water. Paint them when they are quite cold, using felt pens (see page 92). Cover them completely with different designs, shading in some areas, drawing flowers or simple stripes and geometric patterns. Your aim will be to get as much variety as possible.

Another way is to draw on your designs with a wax pencil, then boil the eggs in a dye. The design will stand out as delicate tracery.

Egg-decorating could even be one of your party activities (see page 14). In that case of course you just prepare the eggs and leave your friends to do the rest, with a plentiful supply of felt pens or paints and brushes.

Yet another way of decorating eggs – and a way that makes it possible to keep them for as long as you like afterwards – is to blow out the contents. This would fit in well with a party where scrambled eggs are on the menu! Prick a hole at each end of the egg with a darning needle, and blow gently from the thin end. Handling the shells carefully, you and your guests then decorate them, using gum and a supply of beads, seeds, dried grasses and flowers, sequins and anything else that is small and decorative from your Bit Box (see page 93).

Mobiles

A wire clothes-hanger makes a good base (see page 94). From it hang different lengths of very fine wire or strong thread. Draw and paint (on both sides of the paper) characters suited to your party. For a Nursery Rhyme Party, for instance, you could use Little Bo-peep and all her sheep. Make a hole at the top of each picture, thread a length of the wire or cotton through it, and knot. Then find somewhere to hang your mobile.

'*Then Tigger looked up at the ceiling, and closed his eyes, and his tongue went round and round his chops, in case he had left any outside, and a peaceful smile came over his face.*'
The House at Pooh Corner

Chapter Five

Suggestions for Food and Drink

Everyone looks forward to the food at a party, and here are some special ideas for cold sandwiches, hot dishes, salads, dessert squares and easy-to-make jelly. You could choose one from each section to make your own party menu. Or combine them with recipes you already know. If you don't want to cook, add a few sandwich ideas of your own to the special recipes given here. If it's cold weather and you have been outside for some of your party it might be a good idea to have a choice of hot dishes, plus a hot drink. Of course, if you are off on a picnic you need to make things that can be packed into a basket, and the recipe for Picnic Tubs is perfect for that. If you want additional ideas that you can easily make yourself, THE POOH COOK BOOK by Katie Stewart is filled with recipes for all occasions.

In general, allow four slices of bread for each person (including what you use in sandwiches), two or three sausages (more if they are little ones), three small cakes, five biscuits, and one portion of jelly or ice-cream. If you are cooking out allow two hot dogs per person, or one or two hamburgers depending on the size, or a piece of cold chicken each. Allow the equivalent of a small packet of crisps per person. As for drinks, a bottle of fruit squash is enough for six to eight people, a bottle of fizzy drink for two.

Cool and Easy

These two special sandwich recipes can, of course, be used with your own favourites. Perhaps you are fond of cheese and chutney, or egg-mayonnaise, or banana sandwiches but would like to try something new. These are not difficult and look so partyish when arranged on a large plate.

Sardine and Lemon Fingers

>   2 tablespoons lemon juice
>   1 can (about 4 oz) drained sardines
>   4 oz (or 4 rounded tablespoons) butter, softened
>   1 egg, separated
>   Salt and pepper
>   1 level tablespoon chopped parsley
>   Slices of buttered bread, with crusts off
>   and cut into fingers

Squeeze out the juice from half a lemon. Mash the sardines finely with a fork. Stir in one tablespoon of lemon juice and beat in the butter. Add the egg yolk, salt, pepper and parsley and another tablespoon of lemon juice if necessary. Beat the egg white until it is stiff and fold it into the mixture gently with a wooden spoon. Serve on fingers of bread spread with butter.

Peanut Butter Chunks

>   3 slices white bread
>   3 slices brown bread
>   Plenty of peanut butter, according to taste

First cut off the crusts. Then, arranging bread colours alternately, spread five of the slices thickly with peanut butter, and top with

the sixth. Press together, wrap in cellophane, and put in refrigerator or a cold place to chill. When ready to serve slice down
in three equal portions. Now cut across these three portions in the
other direction, three times again. Arrange the resulting long
chunky 'sandwiches' on a plate, in a circle, and garnish with
chopped mint or parsley. These also taste very good when made
with cream cheese.

Hot and Tasty

For a cold weather party, or as a savoury dish in addition to
sandwiches, here are three very tasty and filling dishes. Baked
beans or scrambled eggs on toast are always popular after a
winter outing as well.

Little Meat Balls

(makes 40–50 bite-size balls)
  1 lb lean minced beef
  1 small minced onion
  Garlic powder (optional)
  Salt and pepper
  A little beaten egg, if necessary, to bind
  Butter for frying

Mix meat, onion, garlic and seasoning well together, and if the
mixture doesn't quite cling together add a little beaten egg until
it *does*. Pull off tiny pieces, roll into small balls. Melt the butter
slowly in a pan and fry the meatballs in it, over medium heat,
till golden brown all over. Be careful that the butter doesn't
become too hot and burn. These can be made ahead of time and
re-heated; or you can serve them cold, speared on cocktail sticks
or wooden toothpicks.

Sausage and Chutney Surprise

(Makes 8)
    8 fairly thin slices bread
    8 skinless sausages
    Butter
    Favourite chutney

Cut the crusts from the bread, and since it is to be rolled, flatten it a little first with a rolling pin. Spread the slices of bread with softened butter. Cover with your favourite chutney. Put a skinless sausage at the end of each bread slice. Roll up the bread neatly, and secure each roll with a wooden toothpick. Grease a baking sheet. Put the rolls on this, and spread outsides with a little more soft butter. Bake in fairly hot oven (375° F, Gas Mark 5) on the shelf next to the top, for about 25–30 minutes. If the bread starts to get too brown before this time, bring farther down the oven. These are also delicious eaten cold.

Cheese and Bacon Rolls

    8 crusty rolls
    1 family-size can baked beans
    4 oz (4 heaped tablespoons) strong Cheddar cheese
    4 large rashers bacon, chopped in small pieces.

Cut a lid off the top of each roll. Using your fingers, pull out the bread centres (keep the bread centres for use later for bread sauce or rissoles etc.). Brush the outside of each roll with a little cooking oil. Now fill the hollows of the rolls with baked beans.

Grate the cheese and then divide this between each roll, spooning it on top of the beans. Top with a few bacon pieces. Cover each roll with its 'lid', put on baking tray, and bake in a hot oven (375° F or Gas Mark 5) for 30 minutes.

Simple Salads

For picnics, or perhaps summer parties, salads look crisp and cool and can be made ahead. You can always add celery, carrot, and cucumber sticks – radishes as well, or perhaps washed lettuce, carried in a sturdy plastic bag from which everyone can help themselves on a picnic.

I'd made up a little basket, just a little, fair sized
basket, an ordinary biggish sort of basket full of –
The House at Pooh Corner

Curried Party Eggs

12 eggs, hardboiled – shelled
2 packets cream cheese (the 3 oz size)
Seasoning to taste – salt,
   pepper, and curry powder
Little snippets of cucumber, tomato
   parsley, radish or carrot

Cut the eggs in half. Remove the yolks, being careful not to split the whites. Put the yolks in a small bowl, mash them with a fork, and add the cream cheese. Put the curry powder in a little at a time, and the salt and pepper, until it tastes the way you like it. Mix well. Now pile the mixture back into the egg white cases. Decorate the tops, and place on a platter with lettuce leaves. If it is a picnic a cardboard box would be useful for packing the eggs between layers of greaseproof paper.

Picnic Tubs

If you save individual plastic tubs, the kind that margarines and yoghurts come in, you can use them as picnic containers for individual portions of salad to be eaten with a fork or spoon. Here is one Picnic Tub salad suggestion that gives eight large (or more smaller) servings.

3 lb new potatoes, cooked and diced
1 lb pork sausages, cooked and sliced
2 eating apples, cored and chopped
4 tablespoons lemon juice
4 in. length of cucumber, diced
2 oz salted peanuts
4 spring onions, chopped
Sprigs of watercress

Sprinkle the apple pieces with lemon juice. Put them into a bowl, along with everything else (except the watercress). Chill in a cold place, then pack into the containers and garnish each with a sprig of watercress. These can be taken on a picnic, but remember the forks, and have a bottle of salad cream handy if you like.

Delicious Desserts

It is always nice to have a choice for dessert. If it is a birthday party naturally the cake is most important. A very special cake can be found in THE POOH COOK BOOK. For other occasions you might like to make one of the following recipes to serve with ice cream. Or perhaps you have a recipe for biscuits that you especially like, and you could make these as well as *Tilted Jellies*.

Honey-nut Squares

　　8 oz plain biscuits, broken into small pieces
　　3 oz butter (and a little extra for greasing tin)
　　6 level tablespoons thick honey
　　4 level tablespoons crunchy peanut butter

Grease a shallow 7 inch square tin with butter. Put the 3 oz butter in a saucepan. Measure honey into the same pan. Place the pan over low heat and bring to the boil, stirring carefully. Remove the pan from the heat and mix in the peanut butter: add broken biscuits and mix well. Place the mixture in the greased tin and press down with the back of a dessertspoon. Leave in a cool place till it's firm. Then cut into sixteen squares.

Krispie Shortbread

For the shortbread:
　　4 oz butter
　　2 oz (2 rounded tablespoons) caster sugar
　　4 oz (4 rounded tablespoons) cornflour
　　2 oz (2 rounded tablespoons) plain flour

For the topping:

　　2 oz plain chocolate
　　1 oz butter
　　3 tablespoons golden syrup
　　2 oz Rice Krispies

Cream butter and sugar until light and fluffy. Sieve cornflour and flour together and gradually work into the creamed mixture. Knead mixture until smooth. Press into 8 inch round loose-bottomed cake tin. Prick all over with fork. Bake in slow oven (325° F or Mark 3) for 40–45 minutes. Remove from oven and cover immediately with hot Krispie topping. The topping will take about 10 minutes to make. This is how you do it. Melt chocolate, butter and syrup together in a saucepan. Remove from heat and stir in Rice Krispie. Make sure Rice Krispies are evenly coated with chocolate. While still hot, use to top the shortbread. If the topping has cooled it can be reheated over a low flame.

Remove from the tin when cold and cut into portions. Ask an adult to help cut it carefully with a sharp knife as the shortbread breaks easily.

Tilted Jellies

(Serves 10)
    1 pint red jelly
    1 pint yellow jelly
    1 large can fruit cocktail
    Canned or fresh cream for decoration (optional)

Make the red jelly according to packet directions and divide equally between 10 tall glasses. Put the glasses in the refrigerator to set, but tilt each of them at an angle (resting them against the walls of the refrigerator – carefully wedging the glasses in the grooves of shelves). When red jelly is completely set, make up the yellow jelly and allow this to become cold but not set. Pour into glasses on top of the red jelly and leave to set in the refrigerator, this time tilting the glasses in the opposite direction. When it is completely set, fill up the glasses with fruit cocktail. (Cream, too, if you like).

Drinks with-a-difference

Drinks can be an important part of the menu, especially when they are as tasty and unusual as some of these recipes. Part of the fun is the mashing, the mixing and the whipping up. You could even make delicious drinks the reason for a party.

Hunny Froth

(Serves 4)
A drink that would definitely win Pooh's approval.
   4 ripe bananas
   4 tablespoons thin honey
   4 tablespoons fresh orange juice
   1 pint milk
   Cake decorations (multi-coloured)

Mash the bananas, and beat together with the orange juice and honey. Whisk in the milk. When frothy, serve in glasses, sprinkling tops with tiny coloured cake decorations.

Butterscotch Whirl

(Serves 4)

    3 teaspoons chocolate spread
    3 teaspoons golden syrup
    1½ pints chilled milk
    6 level dessertspoons butterscotch-flavoured instant
      whip powder
    Finely chopped walnuts

Mix the chocolate spread with the syrup. Then, using a teaspoon, spread this mixture round the inside of 4 glasses. Make up the instant whip following the basic packet directions but using the quantities of milk and powder given above. Just before serving whisk well and pour the mixture carefully into the glasses. Add straws, and serve sprinkled with chopped walnuts.

Blackcurrant and Vanilla Froth

(Serves 4)

    1½ pints milk
    6 tablespoons blackcurrant syrup
    Vanilla ice cream (about 4 average portions)

Simply whisk everything together in a bowl just as hard as you can, with a beater or an electric blender. Pour into glasses or beakers, and serve with straws.

Hot Chocolate Mallow

(Serves 3)

    1 pint milk
    6 heaped teaspoons instant Chocolate drink
    6 marshmallows, chopped

Bring the milk to the boil, and pour into 3 mugs, depending on size. Add 2–3 teaspoons of Chocolate drink to each mug and stir well. Top each mug with chopped marshmallows and serve.

Yoghurt Cooler

(Serves 6)

    1½ pints milk
    3 (6 oz) cartons fruit yoghurt –
    raspberry, apricot, or strawberry
    6 pink marshmallows

Pour the milk into a large jug and add the yoghurt. Whisk together for about half a minute, or until nice and frothy on top. Pour mixture into six glasses, and spoon froth on top of each glass. Cut the marshmallows into quarters with scissors. Float four pieces on each glass. Serve straight-away with straws as well as spoons.

Later on, when they had all said 'Goodbye' and 'Thank You' to Christopher Robin, Pooh and Piglet walked home thoughtfully together in the golden evening.
Winnie-the-Pooh

Metric Conversion Table

The following list shows the Imperial measures used in the recipes in this book and their equivalent metric measures balanced to the nearest 5 grammes. If you prefer to work with metric measures you may like to use these as a guide.

Dry Measures

$\frac{1}{4}$ oz	10 grammes
$\frac{1}{2}$ oz	15 grammes
1 oz	30 grammes
$1\frac{1}{2}$ oz	45 grammes
2 oz	55 grammes
3 oz	85 grammes
4 oz	115 grammes
5 oz	140 grammes
6 oz	170 grammes
7 oz	200 grammes
8 oz	225 grammes
12 oz	340 grammes
1 lb	455 grammes
2 lb	910 grammes

Liquid measures

$\frac{1}{4}$ pint	142 millilitres
$\frac{1}{3}$ pint	189 millilitres
$\frac{1}{2}$ pint	284 millilitres
1 pint	568 millilitres
2 pints	1,136 millilitres

For the Diagrams: one inch equals approximately two and a half centimetres.

How to make costumes and decorations

Pooh Costumes

1   Ears

What you need: Thin card or stiff paper, poster colours or cloth of different colours and gum or a quick-drying clear adhesive, elastic, a stapler or needle and thread, scissors. (See page 50.)

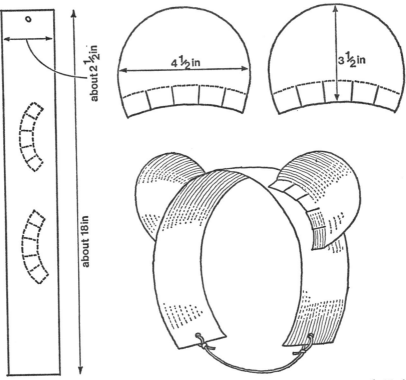

For Pooh, cut out the ears and headband from thin card. Fold back the tabs on the ears and staple, sew or stick them to the headband along the dotted lines. Tie elastic through the holes.

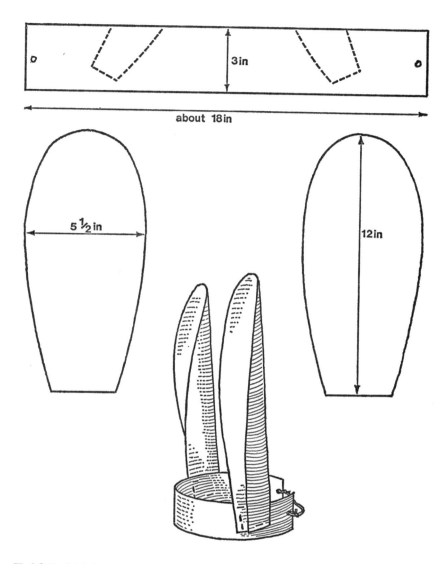

Fold Rabbit's ears as shown (but do not crease them.) Then fix them to the headband. Eeyore's ears are the same shape but should be made from floppy material.

2   Kanga's Apron

What you need: White cotton material, tape, needle and thread, pins, scissors. (See page 51).

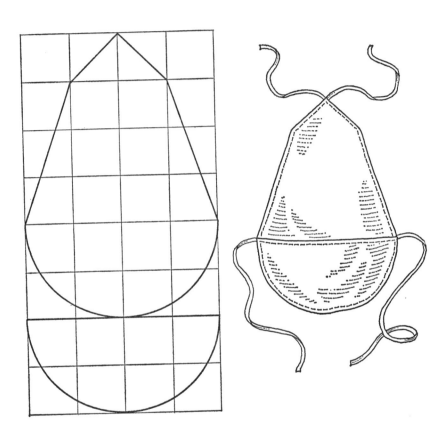

It might be best to make the pattern from newspaper first, to be sure it is right. Then pin the pattern to the cloth and cut round it. Hem the edges of the apron and sew on the pocket and tapes.

3   *Owl*

What you need: A paper bag big enough to go over your head, brown paper, felt pens, scissors and gum. (See page 51).

Put the bag over your head and decide where the eyes ought to go. Then take it off, cut the holes, and draw Owl's face.

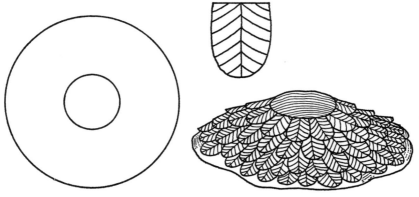

Cut out a collar from brown paper. Draw feathers on it with a felt pen, or make separate feathers and stick them on.

Party Hats

What you need: Margarine containers, elastic, coloured felt pens, gold and silver foil, crepe or other coloured paper, cord, scissors, gum.

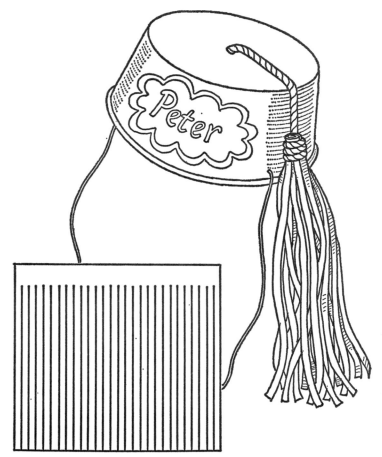

Make holes on each side and thread elastic through, knotting the ends. The tassel is made by fringing crepe paper, rolling it and tying with a coloured cord which goes through a hole in the base of the container.

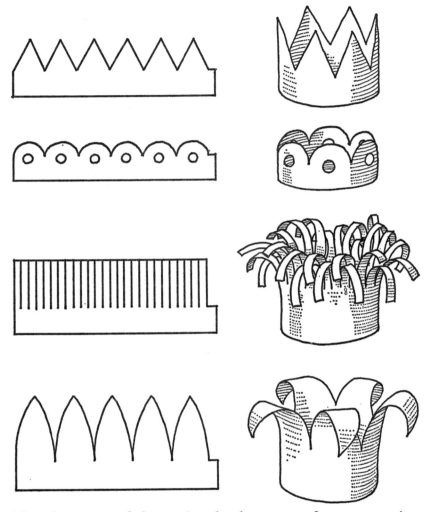

These hats are made by cutting the shapes out of crepe paper (see page 52) then overlapping the ends of each and sticking them together. You can make the fringe and points curl over by stroking each strip of paper on one side with the scissors blade or a ruler.

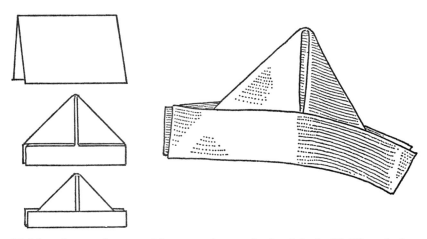

Fold a sheet of paper (about 17 by 24 inches) in half. Then bring the corners of the fold to the centre, and fold up the edges of the paper. Stick if necessary.

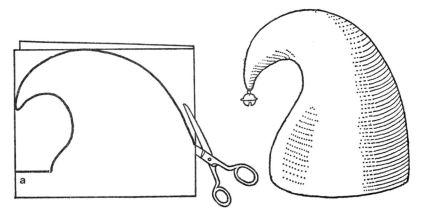

Fold crepe paper (about 10 by 24 inches) in half. Cut the shape through both halves together. Overlap and stick the tabs at *a* to make a headband. Gum the pointed tops together along the edges. The points can be stuffed with lightly crumpled paper scraps.

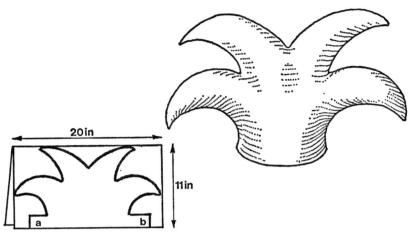

This hat is made in much the same way as the one on the previous page, but the tabs at both *a* and *b* must be overlapped and stuck together.

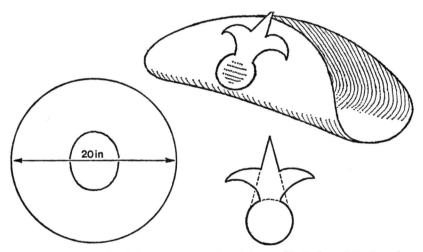

You will need stiff paper to make this soldier's hat. Notice that the edges are stuck together *only* at the top. The badge should be cut from gold paper.

Witch's Hat

Make this witch's hat from stiff paper, but cut the pattern first from newspaper to be sure it fits. (See page 53). First make the cone by cutting a quarter-circle from a 15 inch square of paper, overlapping and sticking the straight edges together. The brim must have tabs which you can bend up and glue inside the cone.

Masks

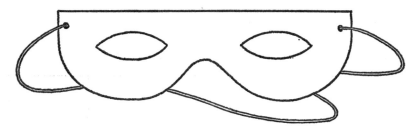

A domino mask is easy to make by cutting this shape from felt or stiff paper. Thread elastic through the holes at the sides. (See page 54).

You can make a mask from a large picnic plate by cutting holes for eyes, nose and mouth. Then paint on other features. Tie elastic through a hole at each side. (See page 54.)

Party Decorations

I   Friezes

What you need: Coloured paper, felt pens, scissors.

Fold a long strip of paper carefully, first one way then the other, so that the folds are an equal distance apart. Draw Pooh or some other character on the top section (see page 55). Then hold all the layers of paper firmly together and cut round the outline.

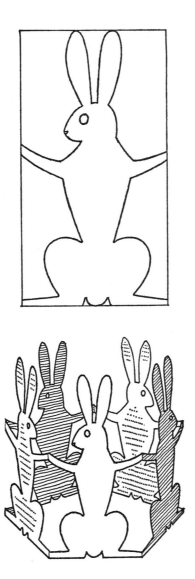

If a frieze is not cut away at the bottom, the ends can be joined to make a circle and it will stand on its own.

2   *Place-markers*

What you need: Thin card, felt pens, scissors.

Fold a piece of card, about 2½ by 5 inches, in half. Draw your design on the lower half. Cut through both front and back together to shape the sides. (See page 56.)

3 *A Centrepiece for the Table*

What you need: Green felt or crepe paper, plasticine, model animals, fences etc., twigs, a small mirror, scissors.

Cut a hole in the felt or crepe paper for the pond and put a small mirror under it. Make banks from plasticine and push in twigs for trees. Then arrange the fences and animals. (See page 57).

Decorating Eggs
1   Coloured Designs

What you need: Felt pens, wax crayon, paints and brushes. (See page 58.)

Hard boil the eggs and wait until they are cold before you draw the designs. Or you can draw the designs with wax crayons and then boil the eggs in a dye. The dye will not colour the eggs where there are crayon marks.

2   *Other Decorations*

What you need: A darning needle, beads, seeds, dried grasses, ferns or flowers, sequins, gummed shapes, pasta shapes, or anything that is small and decorative, gum.

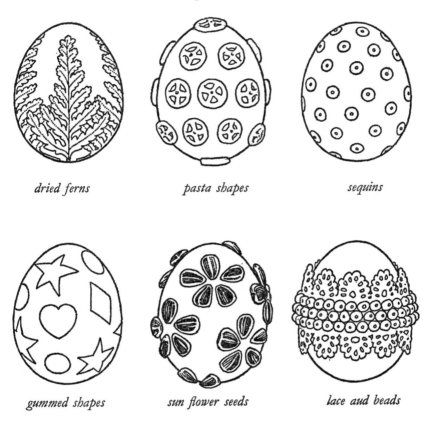

dried ferns   pasta shapes   sequins

gummed shapes   sun flower seeds   lace aud beads

Blow the eggs (see page 58). Then stick the decorations in position with gum.

Mobiles

What you need: a wire clothes-hanger, thin card, felt pens or paint and brushes, cotton, scissors.

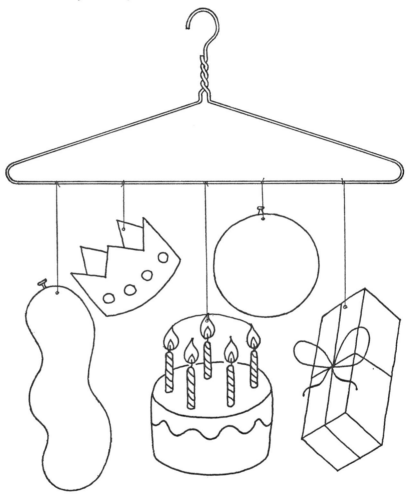

Mobile for a birthday party. Draw the various objects on card and cut them out. Then colour both sides. Make a small hole at the top of each and tie on lengths of cotton thread to suspend them from the clothes-hanger. (See page 58.)

Index